शिवसूत्र

śivasūtra

The Shiva Sutra of Vasugupta

शिवसूत्र

śivasūtra

The Shiva Sutra of Vasugupta

Sanskrit with Transliteration
and English Translation

Gerard D. C. Kuiken

Also by the Author

Thermodynamics of Irreversible Processes, John Wiley, 1994
Eastern Thought and the Gita, OTAM Books, 2012
The Original Gita: Striving for Oneness, Motilal Banarsidass, 2012, 2015
Kashmiri Gitasara, OTAM Books, 2019, 2023
The Roots of the Bhagavadgītā, Volumes I, II, III, OTAM Books, 2023

The Shiva Sutra of Vasugupta

Publisher: OTAM Books
Website: www.gdckuiken.com
Email: g.d.c.kuiken@planet.nl for comments and corrections

ISBN 978-90-78623-14-4

Cover design: Margaret Kay Dodd, Studio K Arts, USA
Email: studiokarts@earthlink.net

Printed in the USA

Contents

Acknowledgments

I would like to express my thanks to Greg Hillis Ph.D., University of California Santa Barbara, for giving me the *Śivasūtravārtika* by Bhāskara in Sanskrit. I gratefully acknowledge Dr. Kuldip Kumar Dhiman, author of *The Yogavāsiṣṭha: The Mind and Its Creation*, for his critical reading of my translation and suggestions for improvement.

Abbreviations

abl., ablative case
acc., accusative case
act., active voice
caus., causative
cpd, compound
DV cpd, Dvandva (copulative) compound
du., dual
esp., especially
f., feminine gender
gen., genitive case
ibc., in the beginning of a compound
ifc., *in fini compositi* or 'at the end of a compound'
ind., indeclinable
indic., indicative mood
inst., instrumental case
loc., locative case
m., masculine gender
mid., middle voice
n., neuter gender
nom., nominative case
opt., optative mood
pl., plural
pr., present tense
sg., singular
TP cpd, Tatparuṣa compound
1st, first person
2nd, second person
3rd, third person
√, verb root
->, changed into

Sanskrit Alphabetic Sequence

a ā i ī u ū ṛ ṝ ḷ e ai o au ṃ ḥ k kh g gh ṅ c ch j jh ñ
ṭ ṭh ḍ ḍh ṇ t th d dh n p ph b bh m y r l v s ś ṣ h

Introduction

Why a new translation? My good friend Ravi Ravindra introduced me to the *Shiva Sutra* during a course in Ojai, California in April 2014. Another friend, Rick Sharpe, asked me about the quality of the translation of the *Shiva Sutra* used in the course. Looking more carefully at that and other translations, it appears to me that all these translations have added interpretations not found in the Sanskrit text. I have tried to honor the Sanskrit text without adding words. Other meanings of each Sanskrit word, aside from the one I chose for my literal translation, are given. It turns out that not only my translation but also other translations of a number of sutras are quite different from each other. I hope this version contributes to the appreciation of the *Shiva Sutra* and deepens your meditation.

The *Shiva Sutra* was revealed to and written down by Vasugupta (ca 875–925 CE). The Sutra is considered mystical and of divine origin. For Kashmir Śaivism, it is one of the most important key sources. It outlines the teachings of Shaiva non-dualism, where the focus is on attaining the Ultimate Reality in which everything is created and dissolved. This ultimate state is called Param Shiva and is beyond description. For attaining this state of Shiva for those who remember to reside in their own inherent-self-nature, which is of the nature of Shiva, no effort or no way (अनुपाय an-upāya) is needed. For everyone else there are three ways (upāyas) for the attainment of Param Shiva described in the Shiva Sutra. There is no strict order given for meditating on the Sutra. It depends on one's stage of evolution. The 22 sutras in the first chapter correspond with the third stage, which is the way of Shiva (śāmbhavopāya) and refers to the stage of evolution of one who is open to absorb the first sutra: Consciousness – Self. The second chapter of 10 sutras is called the second stage, a stage of evolution of one who is competent (śāktopāya) and restrains his thoughts, maintaining a constant awareness of Shiva. The third chapter of 45 sutras is called the first stage. The way in this stage is seen as fine (āṇavopāya) and corresponds with the usual system of yogic efforts.

1 śāmbhavopāya शाम्भवोपाय *The way of Shiva*

शाम्भव śāmbhava *coming or derived from Shiva, relating or sacred to Shiva.* उपाय upāya *way, a means or expedient (of any kind), that by which one reaches one's aim.*

चैतन्यमात्मा ॥ १-१ ॥
1.1 caitanyam ātmā ||
Consciousness is Self.

चैतन्यम् caitanyam [n. nom. sg. caitanya] *consciousness, intelligence, soul, spirit.* आत्मा ātmā [m. nom. sg. ātman] *self, soul, principle of life and sensation; the individual soul, essence, nature, character.*

ज्ञानं बन्धः ॥ १-२ ॥
1.2 jñānaṃ bandhaḥ ||
Knowledge is bondage.

ज्ञानम् jñānam [n. nom. sg. jñāna] *knowledge, knowing, becoming acquainted with.* बन्धः bandhaḥ [m. nom. sg. bandha] *mundane bondage, attachment to this world; a bond, chain, binding, tying; imprisonment; putting together, uniting, forming.*

योनिवर्गः कलाशरीरम् ॥ १-३ ॥
1.3 yonivargaḥ kalāśarīram ||
The multitude of similar origins is the body of parts of the whole.

योनि yoni [m. TP cpd yoni-] *origin, source, spring; the womb, female organs of generation; seat, abode, place of rest; family, race, caste.* वर्गः vargaḥ [m. nom. sg. TP cpd -varga] *a multitude of similar things (animate or inanimate), a class, family, group.* कला kalā [f. TP cpd kalā-] *any single part or portion of the whole, a sixteenth part; any practical art, any mechanical or fine art.* शरीरम् śarīram [n. nom. sg. TP cpd -śarīra] *the body, bodily frame, solid parts of the body.*

ज्ञानाधिष्ठानं मातृका ॥ १-४ ॥
1.4 jñānādhiṣṭhānaṃ mātṛkā ||
The basis of knowledge is an alphabet.

ज्ञान jñāna [n. TP cpd jñāna-] *knowledge, knowing, becoming acquainted with.* अधिष्ठानम् adhiṣṭhānam [n. nom. sg. TP cpd -adhiṣṭhāna] *a basis, base; site, residence, abode; authority, power.* मातृका mātṛkā [f. nom. sg. mātṛkā] *an alphabet, the totality of letters; mother, divine mother, name of a magical power ascribed to the vowels; that which comes from the mother.*

उद्यमो भैरवः ॥१-५॥
1.5 udyamo bhairavaḥ ||
Zeal is Bhairava.

उद्यमः udyamaḥ [m. nom. sg. ud-yama] *zeal, diligence, perseverance, the act of striving after, exerting one's self, the act of raising or lifting up, elevation; undertaking, beginning.* भैरवः bhairavaḥ [m. nom. sg. bhairava] *Bhairava, a form of Shiva; formidable, frightful, terrible, horrible.*

शक्तिचक्रसंधाने विश्वसंहारः ॥१-६॥
1.6 śakticakrasaṃdhāne viśvasaṃhāraḥ ||
In union of multitude of powers is destruction of the universe.

शक्ति śakti [f. TP cpd śakti-] *power, strength, might, energy, ability, capability, effort; faculty, skill, capacity for.* चक्र cakra [n. TP cpd -cakra-] *a multitude, troop; a wheel, discus, circle.* संधाने saṃdhāne [n. loc. sg. TP cpd -saṃdhāna] *in the union, the act of placing or joining together or uniting; in bringing together.* विश्व viśva [TP cpd viśva-] *all, every, every one; whole, entire, universal; all-pervading or all-containing.* [m.] *the intellectual faculty.* [n.] *the whole world, universe.* संहारः saṃhāraḥ [m. nom. sg. TP cpd -saṃ-hāra] *destruction (esp.) the periodical destruction of the universe at the end of a kalpa; bringing together, collection.*

जाग्रत्स्वप्नसुषुप्तभेदे तुर्याभोगसम्भवः ॥१-७॥
1.7 jāgratsvapnasuṣuptabhede turyābhogasambhavaḥ ||
In the distinction of deep sleep, dreaming and waking is the source of fullness of the Fourth.

जाग्रत् jāgrat [m. DV cpd jāgrat-] *waking.* स्वप्न svapna [m. DV cpd -svapna-] *dreaming; sleep, sleeping; sloth, indolence.* सुषुप्त suṣupta [DV cpd -su-ṣupta-] *deep sleep.* भेदे bhede [m. loc. sg. DV cpd -bheda] *in the distinction, difference, variety; in breaking, splitting, cleaving; in dualism, duality.* तुर्य turya [TP cpd turya-] *being the 4th state of the soul.* [n.] *the Fourth, the 4th state of the soul.* आभोग ābhoga [m. TP cpd -ā-bhoga-] *fullness, circuit, circumference; winding, curving, curve; enjoyment.* सम्भवः sambhavaḥ [m. nom. sg. TP cpd -sam-bhava] *source, origin, birth, production; cause, reason; appearance, occurrence; possibility, ability; existence, being.*

ज्ञानं जाग्रत् ॥१-८ ॥
1.8 jñānaṃ jāgrat ||
Knowledge is waking.

ज्ञानम् jñānam [n. nom. sg. jñāna] *knowledge, knowing, becoming acquainted with.* जाग्रत् jāgrat [m. nom. sg. jāgrat] *waking.*

स्वप्नो विकल्पाः ॥१-९ ॥
1.9 svapno vikalpāḥ ||
Dreaming – imaginations.

स्वप्नः svapnaḥ [m. nom. sg. svapna] *dreaming; sleep, sleeping; indolence, sloth.* विकल्पाः vikalpāḥ [m. nom. pl. vikalpa] *imaginations, false notions, fancies; variations, combinations, diversities, manifoldness; indecisions, irresolutions, doubts, hesitations; alternations, options.*

अविवेको माया सौषुप्तम् ॥१-१० ॥
1.10 aviveko māyā sauṣuptam ||
Non-distinction is deep sleep, which is Maya.

अविवेकः avivekaḥ [m. nom. sg. a-viveka] *non-distinction, non-separation; absence of judgment or discrimination.* माया māyā [f. TP cpd māyā-] *illusion, unreality, deception; art, wisdom, extraordinary or supernational power; duplicity; an unreal or illusory image, phantom, apparition.* सौषुप्तम् sauṣuptam [n. nom. sg. from -su-supta] *deep sleep; fast asleep.*

त्रितयभोक्ता वीरेशः ॥१-११ ॥
1.11 tritayabhoktā vīreśaḥ ||
The Eater of the triad is Shiva. or: *The Enjoyer of the triad is Shiva.*

त्रितय tritaya [n. TP cpd tritaya] *a triad.* भोक्ता bhoktā [m. nom. sg. bhoktṛ] *eater, enjoyer, experiencer, feeler, sufferer; possessor.* वीरेशः vīreśaḥ [m. nom. sg. vīra-iśa] *chief of heroes, a name of Shiva; one who is emancipated to a certain degree; "master of the senses."* (Note: Shiva as destroyer.)

विस्मयो योगभूमिकाः ॥१-१२ ॥
1.12 vismayo yogabhūmikāḥ ||
The stages of yoga are a wonder.

विस्मयः vismayaḥ [m. nom. sg. vismaya] *wonder, surprise, amazement, bewilderment, perplexity* योग yoga [m. TP cpd yoga-] *yoga, union.* भूमिकाः bhūmikāḥ [f. nom. pl. TP cpd -bhūmikā] *(ifc.) (metaphysical) stages, steps, degrees; spots, places for; earths, grounds, soils.*

इच्छा शक्तिरुमा कुमारि ॥१-१३ ॥
1.13 icchā śaktir umā kumāri ||
Desire, power is Uma, the Virgin.

इच्छा icchā [f. TP cpd icchā-] *desire, wish, inclination.* शक्तिः śaktiḥ [f. nom. sg. TP cpd -śakti] *power, strength, might, energy, ability, capability, effort; faculty, skill, capacity for.* उमा umā [f.] *name of the daughter of a wife of Shiva.* कुमारि kumāri [f. short for kumārī] *a virgin, young girl, daughter, maiden.*

दृश्यं शरीरम् ॥१-१४ ॥
1.14 dṛśyaṃ śarīram ||
Any visible object is a body.

दृश्यं dṛśyaṃ [n. nom. sg. dṛśya] *any visible object; visible, conspicuous.* शरीरम् śarīram [n. nom. sg. śarīra] *a body, bodily frame, solid parts of the body.*

हृदये चित्तसङ्घट्टाद्दृश्यस्वापदर्शनम् ॥ १-१५ ॥
1.15 hṛdaye cittasaṅghaṭṭād dṛśyasvāpadarśanam ||
From the union of the mind in the heart is the appearance of dreams of any visible object.

हृदये hṛdaye [n. loc. sg. hṛdaya] *in the heart (or region of the heart as the seat of feelings and sensations), the soul, the mind (as the seat of mental operations); in the heart or center or core or essence or best or dearest or most secret part of anything.* चित्त citta [n. TP cpd citta-] *the mind, heart; thinking, reflecting, imagining, thought.* सङ्घट्टात् saṅghaṭṭāt [m. abl. sg. TP cpd -saṃghaṭṭa] *from the union or junction with; from rubbing or clashing together, friction, collision, conflict.* दृश्य dṛśya [n. TP cpd dṛśya-] *any visible object; visible, conspicuous.* स्वाप svāpa [m. TP cpd -svāpa-] *dream, dreaming; sleeping, sleep.* दर्शनम् darśanam [n. nom. sg. TP cpd -darśana] *(ifc.) appearance, aspect, semblance; seeing, observing, looking, noticing, observation, perception; view, doctrine; the becoming visible or known, presence; vision.*

शुद्धतत्त्वसंधानाद्वापशुशक्तिः ॥ १-१६ ॥
1.16 śuddhatattvasaṃdhānād vāpaśuśaktiḥ ||
Or from the union with the Pure Principle without the power of animals.

शुद्ध śuddha [TP cpd śuddha-] *clean, pure, free from; genuine, true.* तत्त्व tattva [n. TP cpd -tattva-] *a true principle; true or real state, truth, reality.* संधानात् saṃdhānāt [n. abl. sg. TP cpd -saṃdhāna] *from the union, the act of placing or joining together or uniting.* वा vā [ind.] *or.* अ a *a prefix having a negative or privative or contrary sense.* पशु paśu [m. TP cpd paśu-] *any animal; cattle, a domestic or sacrificial animal.* शक्तिः śaktiḥ [f. nom. sg. TP cpd -śakti] *power, strength, might, energy, ability, capability, effort; faculty, skill, capacity for.*

वितर्क आत्मज्ञानम् ॥ १-१७ ॥
1.17 vitarka ātmajñānam ||
Reflection is knowledge of the self.

वितर्कः vitarkaḥ [m. nom. sg. vitarka] *reflection, conjecture, imagination, supposition, guess, opinion.* आत्मा ātmā [m. TP cpd ātman-] *the self, individual soul, essence, nature, character, the soul, principle of life and sensation.* ज्ञानम् jñānam [n. nom. sg. -jñāna] *knowledge, knowing, becoming acquainted with.*

लोकानन्दः समाधिसुखम् ॥१-१८ ॥
1.18 lokānandaḥ samādhisukham ||
Pure happiness of the world is joy of contemplation.

लोक loka [m. TP cpd loka-] *the wide space or world; the earth or world of human beings; mankind, people; ordinary life, worldly affairs.* आनन्दः ānandaḥ [m. nom. sg. TP cpd -ānanda] *pure happiness (an attribute of ātman in vedānta); happiness, joy, enjoyment.* समाधि samādhi [m. TP cpd sam-ādhi-] *intense contemplation of any particular object; intense application or fixing the mind on; concentration of thoughts, profound or abstract meditation.* सुखम् sukham [n. nom. sg. TP cpd -sukha] *joy, ease, pleasure, happiness.*

शक्तिसंधाने शरीरोत्पत्तिः ॥१-१९ ॥
1.19 śaktisaṃdhāne śarīrotpattiḥ ||
In the union of power is the origin of bodies.

शक्ति śakti [f. TP cpd śakti-] *power, strength, might, energy, ability, capability, effort; faculty, skill, capacity for.* संधाने saṃdhāne [n. loc. sg. TP cpd -saṃdhāna] *in the union, the act of placing or joining together or uniting; in bringing together.* शरीर śarīra [n. TP cpd śarīra-] *the body, bodily frame, solid parts of the body.* उत्पत्तिः utpattiḥ [f. nom. sg. TP cpd -utpatti] *origin, arising, birth, production.*

भूतसंधानभूतपृथक्त्वविश्वसङ्घट्टाः ॥१-२० ॥
1.20 bhūtasaṃdhānabhūtapṛthaktvaviśvasaṅghaṭṭāḥ ||
Union of elements, separateness of elements, and all-pervading union.

भूत bhūta [n.] *an element; that which is or exists, the world, any living being; a spirit, a demon.* संधान saṃdhāna [n.] *the union, the act of placing or joining together or uniting; bringing together.* भूत bhūta [n.] *element.* पृथक्त्व pṛthaktva [n. pṛthak-tva] *separateness, separately, the quality of being widely apart.* विश्व viśva [m.] *all-pervading or all-containing;*

all, every, every one; whole, entire, universal; the intellectual faculty. [n.] *the whole world, universe.* सङ्घट्टाः saṅghaṭṭāḥ [m. nom. pl. DV cpd -saṃghaṭṭa] *the union or junction with; rubbing or clashing together, friction, collision, conflict.*

शुद्धविद्योदयाच्चक्रेशत्वसिद्धिः ॥ १-२१ ॥
1.21 śuddhavidyodayāc cakreśatvasiddhiḥ ||
Fulfilment of being the lord of the world is from rising of pure knowledge.

शुद्ध śuddha [TP cpd śuddha-] *pure, clean, free from; genuine, true.* विद्या vidyā [f. TP cpd -vidyā-] *knowledge, science, learning, scholarship, philosophy.* उदयात् udayāt [m. abl. sg. TP cpd -udaya] *from rising, coming forth, appearance; from production, creation.* चक्रेश cakreśa [n. cakra-īśa] *the lord of the world.* चक्र cakra [n.] *wheel, circle, multitude.* ईश īśa *lord, master, ruler.* त्व tva *(as a suffix to nouns expresses) the state or condition of being.* सिद्धिः siddhiḥ [f. nom. sg. siddhi] *fulfilment, accomplishment; prosperity, fortune, advantage; the acquisition of supernatural powers.*

महाह्रदानुसंधानान्मन्त्रवीर्यानुभवः ॥ १-२२ ॥
1.22 mahāhradānusaṃdhānānān mantravīryānubhavaḥ ||
From investigation of the great deep water is the experience of the energy of mantras.

महा mahā [(ibc.) for mahat] *great, large, big, eminent, long, high, important.* ह्रद hrada [m.] *a large or a deep piece of water, lake, pool.* अनुसंधानानात् anusaṃdhānānāt [n. abl. sg. anu-saṃdhānāna] *from investigation, inquiry, arranging, planning.* मन्त्र mantra [m.] *"instrument of thought," speech, sacred text or speech, a prayer or song of praise; a Vedic hymn or sacrificial formula; a sacred formula addressed to any individual deity; a mystical verse or magical formula, incantation; consultation, resolution, secret.* वीर्य vīrya [n.] *energy, manliness, strength, power; manly vigor, virility.* अनुभवः anubhavaḥ [m. nom. sg. anubhava] *experience, knowledge derived from personal observation or experiment.*

2 śāktopāya The way of the competent one

शक्त śakta *able, competent for, equal to, capable of.* उपाय upāya *way, a means or expedient (of any kind), that by which one reaches one's aim.*

चित्तं मन्त्रः ॥ २-१ ॥
2.1 cittaṃ mantraḥ ||
Mind is a mantra.

चित्तम् cittam [n. nom. sg. citta] *the mind, heart; thinking, reflecting, imagining, thought.* मन्त्रः mantraḥ [m. nom. sg. mantra] *"instrument of thought," speech, sacred text or speech, a prayer or song of praise; a Vedic hymn or sacrificial formula; a sacred formula addressed to any individual deity; a mystical verse or magical formula, incantation; consultation, resolution, secret, counsel, advice, plan, design.*

प्रयत्नः साधकः ॥ २-२ ॥
2.2 prayatnaḥ sādhakaḥ ||
Persevering effort is fulfilling.

प्रयत्नः prayatnaḥ [m. nom. sg. prayatna] *persevering effort, endeavor or continued exertion, exertion betowed on, activity, action, act.* साधकः sādhakaḥ [m. nom. sg. sādhaka] *fulfilling, effective, efficient, accomplishing, perfecting, finishing; an efficient or skilful person, (esp.) an adept.*

विद्याशरीरसत्ता मन्त्ररहस्यम् ॥ २-३ ॥
2.3 vidyāśarīrasattā mantrarahasyam ||
The being of the body of knowledge is the secret of a mantra.

विद्या vidyā [f. TP cpd vidyā-] *knowledge, science, learning, scholarship, philosophy.* शरीर śarīra [n. TP cpd śarīra-] *the body, bodily frame, solid parts of the body.* सत्ता sattā [f. nom. sg. TP cpd -sat-tā] *existence, being.* मन्त्र mantra [m. mantra-] *"instrument of thought," speech, sacred text or speech, a prayer or song of praise; a Vedic hymn or sacrificial formula; a sacred formula addressed to any individual deity; a mystical verse or magical formula, incantation; consultation, resolution, secret.* रहस्यम् rahasyam [n. nom. sg. TP cpd rahasya] *a secret, any secret doctrine or mystery, any subtle point, mystical or esoteric teaching; mysterious, concealed.*

गर्भे चित्तविकासोऽविशिष्टविद्यास्वप्नः ॥ २-४ ॥
2.4 garbhe cittavikāso 'viśiṣṭavidyāsvapnaḥ ||
Development of the mind in the womb is a dream of indistinct knowledge.

गर्भे garbhe [m. loc. sg. garbha] *in the womb, a foetus or embryo, child; in the inside, middle, interior of anything.* चित्त citta [n. TP cpd citta-] *the mind, heart; thinking, reflecting, imagining, thought.* विकासः vikāsaḥ [m. nom. sg. TP cpd -vikāsa] *expanding, budding; opening (of the heart), cheerfulness, serenity; expansion, development, growth.* अविशिष्ट aviśiṣṭa [TP cpd -a-viśiṣṭa-] *indistinct, inferior, indistinguished.* विद्या vidyā [f. TP cpd -vidyā-] *knowledge, science, learning, scholarship, philosophy.* स्वप्नः svapnaḥ [m. nom. sg. svapna] *a dream, dreaming; sleep, sleeping.*

विद्यासमुत्थाने स्वाभाविके खेचरी शिवावस्था ॥ २-५ ॥
2.5 vidyāsamutthāne svābhāvike khecarī śivāvasthā ||
Flying the state of Shiva is in the rising of knowledge arising from one's own nature.

विद्या vidyā [f. TP cpd -vidyā-] *knowledge, science, learning, scholarship, philosophy.* समुत्थाने samutthāne [n. loc. sg. TP cpd -samutthāna] *in rise, origin ((ifc.) in rising or springing from); in performance of work, active operation, effort, industry.* स्वाभाविके svābhāvike [m./n. loc. sg. svābhāvika] *in belonging to or arising from one's own nature, natural, native, spontaneous, original, pecular, inherent.* खेचरी khecarī [f. nom. sg. khecara] *flying, moving in the air.* शिव śiva [TP cpd śiva-] *auspicious, propitious, gracious, favorable, benign.* [m.] *Shiva, The Auspicious One.* [n.] *welfare, bliss, prosperity.* अवस्था avasthā [f. nom. sg. TP cpd -avasthā] *state, condition; "stability, consistence".* खेचरी शिवावस्था khecarī śivāvasthā *flying the state of Shiva; the stance of flying through the void of the supreme consciousness (Abhinavagupta).*

गुरुरुपायः ॥ २-६ ॥
2.6 gurur upāyaḥ ||
The guru is the means.

गुरुः guruḥ [m. nom. sg. guru] *guru (gu-ru = one who dispels darkness), any venerable or respectable person; a spiritual parent or preceptor; heavy, weighty (opposed to laghu = light, quick, swift, active; easy, not heavy or difficult); difficult to digest; excessive, difficult, hard; important, serious, momentous.* उपायः upāyaḥ [m. nom. sg. upāya] *the means, that by which one reaches one's aim, an expedient (of any kind), way; solution.*

मातृकाचक्रसम्बोधः ॥ २-७ ॥
2.7 mātṛkācakrasambodhaḥ ||
Perfect knowledge of the multitude of letters.

मातृका mātṛkā [f. nom. sg. TP cpd mātṛkā-] *the totality of letters, an alphabet; mother, divine mother, name of a magical power ascribed to the vowels; that which comes from the mother.* चक्र cakra [n. TP cpd -cakra-] *the multitude, a troop; a wheel, discus, circle.* सम्बोधः sambodhaḥ [m. nom. sg. sambodha] *perfect knowledge or understanding.*

शरीरं हविः ॥ २-८ ॥
2.8 śarīraṃ haviḥ ||
The body is an oblation.

शरीरम् śarīram [n. nom. sg. śarīra] *the body, bodily frame, solid parts of the body.* हविः haviḥ [n. nom. sg. havis] *an oblation or burnt offering, anything offered as an oblation with fire.*

ज्ञानमन्नम् ॥ २-९ ॥
2.9 jñānam annam ||
Knowledge is food.

ज्ञानम् jñānam [n. nom. sg. -jñāna] *knowledge, becoming acquainted with, knowing.* अन्नम् annam [n. nom. sg. anna] *food; food in a mystical sense (or the lowest form in which the supreme soul is manifested, the coarsest envelope of the Supreme Spirit).*

विद्यासंहारे तदुत्थस्वप्नदर्शनम् ॥ २-१० ॥
2.10 vidyāsaṃhāre tadutthasvapnadarśanam ||
In the destruction of knowledge is the appearance of dreaming of a coming forth of That.

विद्या vidyā [f. TP cpd vidyā-] *knowledge, science, learning, scholarship, philosophy.* संहारे saṃhāre [m. loc. sg. TP cpd -saṃ-hāra] *in destruction (esp.) the periodical destruction of the universe at the end of a kalpa; in bringing together, collection, accumulation.* तत् tat [n. nom. sg. tad-] *that, this, it; this world.* उत्थ uttha [TP cpd -uttha-] *coming forth, originating, derived from; standing up, rising, arising.* स्वप्न svapna [m. TP cpd -svapna-] *dreaming, a dream; sleep, sleeping.* दर्शनम् darśanam [n. nom. sg. TP cpd -darśana] (ifc.) appearance, aspect, semblance; *seeing, observing, looking, noticing, observation, perception; view, doctrine; the becoming visible or known, presence; vision.*

3 āṇavopāya — The fine way

आणव āṇava *fine, minute.* n. *exceeding smallness.* उपाय upāya *way, a means or expedient (of any kind), that by which one reaches one's aim.*

आत्मा चित्तम् ॥ ३-१ ॥
3.1 ātmā cittam ||
The self is mind.

आत्मा ātmā [m. nom. sg. ātman] *the self, individual soul, essence, nature, character; the soul, principle of life and sensation.* चित्तम् cittam [n. nom. sg. citta] *the mind, heart; thinking, reflecting, imagining, thought.*

ज्ञानं बन्धः ॥ ३-२ ॥
3.2 jñānaṃ bandhaḥ ||
Knowledge is bondage.

ज्ञानम् jñānam [n. nom. sg. jñāna] *(wordly) knowledge, knowing, becoming acquainted with.* बन्धः bandhaḥ [m. nom. sg. bandha] *mundane bondage, attachment to this world; binding, tying, a bond, chain; imprisonment; putting together, uniting, forming.*

कलादीनां तत्त्वानामविवेको माया ॥ ३-३ ॥
3.3 kalādīnāṃ tattvānām aviveko māyā ||
Of the beginnings of any single part of the whole is non-distinction of realities, which is Maya.

कला kalā [f. TP cpd kalā-] *any single part or portion of the whole, a sixteenth part; any practical art, any mechanical or fine art; certain divisions of time.* आदीनाम् ādīnām [m. gen. pl. -ādi] *of the beginnings, (ifc.) of et cetera.* तत्त्वानाम् tattvānām [n. gen. pl. tattva] *of realities, true or real states, truths; of true principles.* अविवेकः avivekaḥ [m. nom. sg. a-viveka] *non-distinction, non-separation; absence of judgment or discrimination.* माया māyā [f. nom. sg. māyā] *Maya, illusion, unreality, deception; art, extraordinary or supernational power, wisdom; duplicity; an unreal or illusory image, phantom, apparition.*

शरीरे संहारः कलानाम् ॥ ३-४ ॥
3.4 śarīre saṃhāraḥ kalānām ||
The destroyer of parts is in a body.

शरीरे śarīre [n. loc. sg. śarīra] *in a body, bodily frame, solid parts of a body.* संहारः saṃhāraḥ [m. nom. sg. saṃ-hāra] *a destroyer; destruction, esp., the periodical destruction of the universe at the end of a kalpa; bringing together, binding together (of hair), collection, accumulation.* कलानाम् kalānām [f. gen. pl. kalā-] *of many parts or portions of the whole, of sixteenth parts.*

नाडीसंहारभूतजयभूतकैवल्यभूतपृथक्त्वानि ॥ ३-५ ॥
3.5 nāḍīsaṃhārabhūtajayabhūtakaivalyabhūtapṛthaktvāni ||
The accumulation of channels, victory over the elements, detachment of the elements, and separateness of the elements.

नाडी nāḍī [f. nāḍī-] *"channels in the body along which subtle forces flow," any pipe or tube, the tubular stalk of any plant or any tubular organ.* संहार

saṃhāra [m. -saṃ-hāra-] *accumulation, bringing together, binding together (of hair), collection; destruction esp., the periodical destruction of the universe at the end of a kalpa; a destroyer.* भूत bhūta [n.] *an element (one of the five elements: ether, air, fire, water, earth); that which is or exists, any living being, the world; a spirit, a demon; the past; reality, fact, an actual occurrence.* जय jaya [m.] *victory, conquest, triumph, winning.* भूत bhūta [n.] *element.* कैवल्य kaivalya [n.] *detachment from the soul from matter or other transmigrations, perfect isolation, abstraction, detachment from other connections, beatitude.* भूत bhūta [n.] *element* पृथक्त्वानि pṛthaktvāni [n. nom. pl. DV cpd pṛthak-tva] *separateness.*

मोहावरणात्सिद्धिः ॥ ३-६ ॥
3.6 mohāvaraṇāt siddhiḥ ||
Fulfilment is from an act of concealing the delusion of mind.

मोह moha [m. moha-] *delusion or darkness of mind; loss of consciousness, bewilderment, perplexity, error, distraction, infatuation, delusion, folly; a swoon, fainting, stupefaction.* आवरणात् āvaraṇāt [n. abl. sg. āvaraṇa] *from the act of concealing, covering, hiding; through a bolt, lock.* सिद्धिः siddhiḥ [f. nom. sg. siddhi] *fulfilment, accomplishment; prosperity, fortune, advantage; the acquisition of supernatural powers.*

मोहजयादनन्तभोगात्सहजविद्याजयः ॥ ३-७ ॥
3.7 mohajayād anantabhogāt sahajavidyājayaḥ ||
Through the conquest of the delusion of mind, through infinite enjoyment is the conquest of natural knowledge.

मोह moha [m. moha-] *delusion or darkness of mind; loss of consciousness, bewilderment, perplexity, error, distraction, infatuation, delusion, folly; a swoon, fainting, stupefaction.* जयात् jayāt [m. abl. sg. -jaya] *from or through conquest, victory, triumph, winning.* अनन्त ananta [m./n. ananta] *infinite, endless, boundless, eternal.* भोगात् bhogāt [m. abl. sg. -bhoga] *through enjoyment, eating, feeding on; through any winding or curve; from coil (of a serpent).* सहज sahaja [TP cpd saha-ja-] *natural (ibc., by birth, 'by nature', 'naturally', 'effortless'); innate, congenital, original.* विद्या vidyā [f. -vidyā-] *knowledge, science, learning, scholarship, philosophy.* जयः jayaḥ [m. nom. sg. -jaya] *conquest, victory, triumph, winning.*

जाग्रद्द्वितीयकरः ॥ ३-८ ॥
3.8 jāgrad dvitīyakaraḥ ||
Waking is the doer of forming the second part of anything.

जाग्रत् jāgrat [m. nom. sg. jāgrat] *waking.* द्वितीय dvitīya [m./n. TP cpd dvitīya-] *forming the second part or half of anything; second.* करः karaḥ [m. nom. sg. TP cpd -kara] *a doer, maker, causer, doing, making, causing, producing; a ray of light, sunbeam, moonbeam.*

नर्तक आत्मा ॥ ३-९ ॥
3.9 nartaka ātmā ||
The dancer is Self.

नर्तकः nartakaḥ [m. nom. sg. nartaka] *dancer, singer, actor.* आत्मा ātmā [m. nom. sg. ātman] *the self, individual soul, essence, nature, character; the soul, principle of life and sensation.*

रङ्गोऽन्तरात्मा ॥ ३-१० ॥
3.10 raṅgo 'ntarātmā ||
The stage is the inner self.

रङ्गः raṅgaḥ [m. nom. sg. raṅga] *stage, a place for public amusement or for dramatic exhibition, theater, play-house, arena, any place of assembly.* अन्तर् antar [ind.] *within, between, amongst, in the middle or interior; (ibc.) interior, internal, intermediate.* आत्मा ātmā [m. nom. sg. ātman] *the self, individual soul, essence, nature, character; the soul, principle of life and sensation.*

प्रेक्षकाणीन्द्रियाणि ॥ ३-११ ॥
3.11 prekṣakāṇīndriyāṇi ||
The spectators are the organs of sense.

प्रेक्षकाणि prekṣakāṇi [n. nom. pl. prekṣaka] *spectators, members of an audience; looking at, viewing or intending to view.* इन्द्रियाणि indriyāṇi [n. nom. pl. indriya] *organs of sense, faculties of sense, senses.*

धीवशात्सत्त्वसिद्धिः ॥ ३-१२ ॥
3.12 dhīvaśāt sattvasiddhiḥ ||
By means of wisdom is fulfilment of true essence.

धी dhī [f.] *wisdom, understanding, intelligence, science, art; meditation, thought (esp.) religious thought, reflection, devotion, prayer; mind.* वशात् vaśāt [m. abl. sg. vaśa] *(ifc.) by means of, by command of, on account of, by force of, according to; from will, wish, desire; power, control.* सत्त्व sattva [n.] *true essence, being, entity, reality, existence, nature, disposition of mind, character; vital breath, life, consciousness, strength of character, energy; the quality of purity or goodness; a creature, animal, living or sentient being.* सिद्धिः siddhiḥ [f. nom. sg. siddhi] *fulfilment, accomplishment; prosperity, fortune, advantage; the acquisition of supernatural powers.*

सिद्धः स्वतन्त्रभावः ॥ ३-१३ ॥
3.13 siddhaḥ svatantrabhāvaḥ ||
One who has attained the highest truth is a free being.

सिद्धः siddhaḥ [m. nom. sg. siddha] *one who has attained the highest object, thoroughly skilled or versed in; any inspired sage or prophet or seer; a siddha or semi-divine being of great purity and perfection and said to possess the eight supernatural faculties; any holy personage or great saint; any great adept in magic or one who has acquired supernatural powers; well-known, notorious, celebrated; prepared, cooked, dressed (as food); perfected, become perfect, beatified.* स्वतन्त्र svatantra [n.] *free, self-dependent, self-willed, independent, uncontrolled; self-dependence, independence, self-will, freedom.* भावः bhāvaḥ [m. nom. sg. bhāva] *being, becoming, existing, occurring, appearance; state, condition, rank; manner of being, nature, temperament, character; any state of mind or body, way of thinking or feeling, sentiment, opinion, intention; love, affection, attachment; the seat of the feelings or affections, heart, soul, mind; that which is or exists, thing or substance, being or living creature.*

यथा तत्र तथान्यत्र ॥ ३-१४ ॥
3.14 yathā tatra tathānyatra ||
As there so elsewhere.

यथा yathā [ind. corr. tathā] *as, in which manner or way, according as, like; that, so that, in order that; because, since.* तत्र tatra [ind. corr. yatra] *so, in that place, there.* तथा tathā [ind.] *in that manner, thus; yes, so be it; so also, in like manner.* अन्यत्र anyatra [ind.] *elsewhere, in another place; otherwise.*

बीजावधानम् ॥ ३-१५ ॥
3.15 bījāvadhānam ||
Attention of origin.

बीज bīja [m.] *origin, any germ, element, primary cause or principle, source; seed, semen, seed-corn, grain.* अवधानम् avadhānam [n. nom. sg. avadhāna] *attention, attentiveness, intentness.*

आसनस्थः सुखं ह्रदे निमज्जति ॥ ३-१६ ॥
3.16 āsanasthaḥ sukhaṃ hrade nimajjati ||
Practising asana he easily immerses in deep water.

आसन āsana [n.] *asana; seat, place, stool; abiding, dwelling; sitting, sitting down; sitting in a particular posture according to the custom of devotee.* स्थः sthaḥ [m. nom. sg. stha] *practicing; abiding, being situated in, existing or being in or on or among, standing, staying; occupied with, engaged in, devoted to performing.* सुखम् sukham [n. nom. sg. TP cpd -sukha] *ease, pleasure, happiness, joy.* ह्रदे hrade [m. loc. sg. hrada] *in a large or deep piece of water, lake, pool.* निमज्जति nimajjati [3rd sg. pr. indic. act. √nimajj] *he immerses or submerges in water, sinks down, dives, sinks or plunges or penetrates into, batthes in; disappears, perishes.*

स्वमात्रानिर्माणमापादयति ॥ ३-१७ ॥
3.17 svamātrānirmāṇam āpādayati ||
One causes the creation of one's own measure.

स्व sva [m.] *one's own, own, etc.; a man of one's own people or tribe; a kinsman, relation, friend.* [n.] *one's self, the Ego; one's own goods, property, wealth.* मात्रा mātrā [f. nom. sg. -mātrā-] *measure of any kind; quantity, size, duration, number, degree; a minute portion, particle, atom; materials, property, goods.* निर्माणम् nirmāṇam [n. nom. sg. -nirmāṇa] *creation, forming, making, creating, work.* आपादयति āpādayati [3rd caus. pr. indic. act. ā-√pad] *one causes to cause, produce, bring near or towards; he causes to enter, bring on, bring into trouble or misfortune.*

विद्याविनाशे जन्मविनाशः ॥ ३-१८ ॥
3.18 vidyāvināśe janmavināśaḥ ||
Not in the destruction of knowledge is the destruction of birth.

विद्या vidyā [f. vidyā-] *(self-) knowledge, science, learning, scholarship, philosophy.* अविनाशे avināśe [m. loc. sg. a-vināśa] *not in the destruction, utter loss, annihilation, decay, death; in non-destruction.* जन्म janma [n. TP cpd janman-] *birth, production.* विनाशः vināśaḥ [m. nom. sg. -vināśa] *destruction, utter loss, annihilation, decay, death.*

कवर्गादिषु माहेश्वर्याद्याः पशुमातरः ॥ ३-१९ ॥
3.19 kavargādiṣu māheśvaryādyāḥ paśumātaraḥ ||
The Energy of Shiva et caetera in the beginnings of the class of gutteral letters are the mothers of animals.

कवर्ग kavarga [m. ka-varga] *the class of gutteral letters.* आदिषु ādiṣu [m. loc. pl. -ādi] *in the beginnings, (ifc.) in beginning with, and so on, et caetera.* माहेश्वरी māheśvarī [f. nom. sg. māheśvarī] *the Energy or Consort of Shiva.* आद्याः ādyāḥ [m. nom. pl. ādi] *(ifc.) et caetera; beginnings.* पशु paśu [m. TP cpd paśu-] *cattle, a domestic or sacrificial animal; any animal.* मातरः mātaraḥ [f. nom. pl. TP cpd -mātṛ] *mothers, all mothers (applicable to animals), divine mothers or personified energies of the principal deities closely connected with the worship of Shiva.*

त्रिषु चतुर्थं तैलवदासेच्यम् ॥ ३-२० ॥
3.20 triṣu caturthaṃ tailavad āsecyam ||
The Fourth should be poured like oil in the Three.

त्रिषु triṣu [m. loc. pl. trayas] *in the three.* चतुर्थम् caturtham [n. nom. sg. caturtha] *the fourth.* तैल taila [n.] *oil.* वत् vat *an affix added to words to imply likeness or resemblance.* आसेच्यम् āsecyam [n. nom. sg. gerundive ā-√sic] *must be or should be poured in, filled up, sprinkled, poured on.*

मग्नः स्वचित्तेन प्रविशेत् ॥ ३-२१ ॥
3.21 magnaḥ svacittena praviśet ||
One should enter with one's own mind immerged.

मग्नः magnaḥ [m. nom. sg. magna] *immersed; sunk, plunged, immersed in; (to be engrossed totally).* स्व sva [m.] *one's own, own, etc.; a man of one's own people or tribe; a kinsman, relation, friend.* [n.] *one's self, the Ego; one's own goods, property, wealth.* चित्तेन cittena [n. instr. sg. citta] *by or with the mind, heart; with thinking, reflecting, imagining, thought; by intention, aim, wish.* प्रविशेत् praviśet [3rd pr. opt. act. pra-√viś] *one should enter, go into, resort to; one should enter upon, undertake, commence, devote one's self to.*

प्राणसमाचारे समदर्शनम् ॥ ३-२२ ॥
3.22 prāṇasamācāre samadarśanam ||
Within the practice of prana is a looking on all with indifferent eyes.

प्राण prāṇa [m.] *prana, the breath of life, breath, respiration, spirit, vitality; vigor, energy, power.* समाचारे samācāre [m. loc. sg. sam-ācāra] *within the practice, procedure, conduct.* समदर्शनम् samadarśanam [n. nom. sg. sama-darśana] *looking on all (things and men) with indifferent or equal eyes (to see all as one).*

मध्येऽवरप्रसवः ॥ ३-२३ ॥
3.23 madhye 'varaprasavaḥ ||
Inferior generation in the space between.

मध्ये madhye [ind.] *within, in the middle, in the midst, between, among.* [n. loc. sg. madhya] *in the space between, the middle of the sky; in the middle, midst, center, inside, interior.* अवर avara *inferior, posterior, hinder, later, last, younger; below; low, mean, unimportant, of small value.* प्रसवः prasavaḥ [m. nom. sg. prasava] *generation, procreation, begetting, conception, delivery, birth, origin; simulation, furtherance, aid; offspring, posterity.*

मात्रास्वप्रत्ययसंधाने नष्टस्य पुनरुत्थानम् ॥ ३-२४ ॥
3.24 mātrāsvapratyayasaṃdhāne naṣṭasya punar utthānam ||
In the act of uniting one's own conception of measures is the act of rising again of the lost.

मात्रा mātrā [f. nom. sg. mātrā-] *measure of any kind; quantity, size, duration, number, degree; a minute portion, particle, atom; materials, property, goods.* स्व sva [-sva-] [m.] *one's own, own, etc.; a man of one's own people or tribe; a kinsman, relation, friend.* [n.] *one's self, the Ego; one's own goods, property, wealth.* प्रत्यय pratyaya [m. -pratyaya-] *conception, assumption, notion, idea; proof, ascertainment; ground, basis, motive or cause of anything; consciousness, understanding, intelligence, intellect.* संधाने saṃdhāne [n. loc. sg. TP cpd -saṃdhāna] *in the act of uniting or placing or joining together, in the union; in bringing together.* नष्टस्य naṣṭasya [m./n. gen. sg. naṣṭa] *of the lost, disappeared, perished, destroyed, invisible; of damaged, corrupted, wasted, unsuccessful, fruitless, in vain.* पुनर् punar [ind.] *again, once more; back, home, in an opposite direction; again and again, repeatedly; further, moreover, besides; however, still.* उत्थानम् utthānam [n. nom. sg. utthāna] *the act of or rising or standing up; leaving off; manly exertion, manhood.*

शिवतुल्यो जायते ॥ ३-२५ ॥
3.25 śivatulyo jāyate ||
He becomes like Shiva.

शिव śiva [śiva-] *auspicious, propitious, gracious, favorable, benign.* [m.] *The Auspicious One, Shiva.* [n.] *welfare, prosperity, bliss.* तुल्यः tulyaḥ [m. nom. sg. tulya] *like, equal to, of the same kind or class or number or value, similar, comparable.* जायते jāyate [3rd pr. indic. mid. √jan] *he becomes, is; he generates, begets, produces, creates, causes; he is born or produced, comes into existence.*

शरीरवृत्तिर्व्रतम् ॥ ३-२६ ॥
3.26 śarīravṛttir vratam ||
Maintenance of the body is a holy practice.

शरीर śarīra [n. TP cpd śarīra-] *the body, bodily frame, solid parts of the body.* वृत्तिः vṛttiḥ [f. nom. sg. vṛtti] *maintenance, subsistance; activity, working; addiction or devotion to, practice; mode of life or conduct, behavior; being, existing, occurring or appearing in.* व्रतम् vratam [n. nom. sg. vrata] *holy practice, religious vow or practice, meritorious act of devotion or austerity, solemn vow, a rule; any vow of firm purpose; sphere of action, function, mode or manner of life.*

कथा जपः ॥ ३-२७ ॥
3.27 kathā japaḥ ||
Conversation is mantra recitation.

कथा kathā [f. nom. sg. kathā] *conversation, speech, talking together; story, tale, fable.* जपः japaḥ [m. nom. sg. japa] *(mantra recitation), muttering prayers, repeating in a murmuring tone passages from scripture or charms or names of a deity.*

दानमात्मज्ञानम् ॥ ३-२८ ॥
3.28 dānam ātmajñānam ||
The act of giving is self-knowledge.

दानम् dānam [n. nom. sg. dāna] *the act of giving; donation, gift.* आत्म ātma [m. TP cpd ātman-] *the self, individual soul, essence, nature, character; the soul, principle of life and sensation.* ज्ञानम् jñānam [n. nom. sg. -jñāna] *knowledge, knowing, becoming acquainted with.*

योऽविपस्थो ज्ञाहेतुश्च ॥ ३-२९ ॥
3.29 yo 'vipastho jñāhetuś ca ||
He who is engaged in guarding sheep and the cause of knowing.

यः yaḥ [m. nom. sg. yad] *who, which, what, whichever, whatever, that.* अवि avi *favorable, kindly disposed.* m./f. *a sheep.* प pa *guarding, protecting, ruling.* स्थः sthaḥ [m. nom. sg. stha] *(only ifc.) engaged in, standing, staying, abiding, being situated in, existing or being in or on or among; occupied with, devoted to performing, practicing.* ज्ञा jñā [f. jña] *knowing, familiar with; intelligent, having a soul, wise.* हेतुः hetuḥ [m.

nom. sg. hetu] *cause of, cause, motive.* च ca [ind.] *and, both, also, moreover, as well as.*

स्वशक्तिप्रचयो विश्वम् ॥ ३-३० ॥
3.30 svaśaktipracayo viśvam ||
The multitude of his own power is all-pervading.

स्व sva [sva-] [m. TP cpd] *his own, own* शक्ति śakti [f. TP cpd -śakti-] *power, strength, might, energy, ability, capability, effort; faculty, skill, capacity for.* प्रचयः pracayaḥ [m. nom. sg. pracaya] *multitude; accumulation, heap, mass, quantity.* विश्वम् viśvam [n. nom. sg. viśva] *all-pervading or all-containing; all, every, every one; whole, entire, universal.* [n.] *the whole world, universe.*

स्थितिलयौ ॥ ३-३१ ॥
3.31 sthitilayau ||
Maintenance of life and dissolution.

स्थिति sthiti [f. sthiti-] *maintenance of life, continued existence; standing, remaining, stay, residence; high position, rank; settled rule, axiom.* लयौ layau [m. nom. du. laya] *dissolution, melting; extinction, destruction, death.*

तत्प्रवृत्तावप्यनिरासः संवेत्तृभावात् ॥ ३-३२ ॥
3.32 tatpravṛttāv apy anirāsaḥ saṃvettṛbhāvāt ||
Also without exclusion, this world and acting are both from the character of one who has consciousness.

तत् tat [n. nom. sg. tad-] *this world; it, that, this.* प्रवृत्तौ pravṛttau [m. nom. du. -pravṛtta] *acting, proceeding.* अपि api *also, and, moreover, besides, surely; sometimes a mere expletive, often used to express emphasis, in the sense of even, also, very.* अनिरासः anirāsaḥ [m. nom. sg. a-nirāsa] *without exclusion, casting or throwing out, expulsion, removal, rejection, contradiction, refutation.* संवेत्तृ saṃvettṛ *one who has consciousness, intellect, knowledge, understanding.* भावात् bhāvāt [m. abl. sg. bhāva] *from the character, nature, manner of being, temperament; from becoming, being, existing, occurring, appearance; from the state, condition, rank.*

सुखासुखयोर्बहिर्मननम् ॥ ३-३३ ॥
3.33 sukhāsukhayor bahir mananam ||
Pleasure and pain is outwards thinking.

सुखासुखयोः sukhāsukhayoḥ [n. nom. du. sukha-asukha] *pleasure and pain, joy and sorrow.* बहिः bahiḥ [ind. bahis] *outwards, out, forth, outside.* मननम् mananam [n. nom. sg. manana] *thinking, meditation, reflection, thought, intelligence, understanding.*

तद्विमुक्तस्तु केवली ॥ ३-३४ ॥
3.34 tadvimuktas tu kevalī ||
But freed from this world is one devoted to the doctrine of the absolute unity of spirit.

तत् tat [n. nom. sg. tad-] *this world; this, it, that.* विमुक्तः vimuktaḥ [m. nom. sg. -vimukta] *freed or delivered or escaped from, set free, liberated (esp.) from mundane existence.* तु tu [ind.] *but, now, then.* केवली kevalī [m. nom. sg. kevalin] *"devoted to the doctrine of the absolute unity of spirit", a meditative ascetic; alone, one, only.*

मोहप्रतिसंहतस्तु कर्मात्मा ॥ ३-३५ ॥
3.35 mohapratisaṃhatas tu karmātmā ||
But one whose character is action is towards forming one mass of delusion.

मोह moha [m. moha-] *delusion, loss of consciousness, bewilderment, perplexity, distraction, infatuation, error; darkness or delusion of mind.* प्रति prati [ind.] *(as a prefix to verbs it expresses) towards, near to.* संहतः saṃhataḥ [m. nom. sg. saṃhata] *forming one mass or body, stuck together, closely joined or united with, keeping together, contiguous, coherent, combined, compacted; becoming solid, compact, firm, hard.* तु tu [ind.] *but, now, then.* कर्मात्मा karmātmā [m. nom. sg. karmātman] *one whose character is action, endowed with principles of action, active, acting.*

भेदतिरस्कारे सर्गान्तरकर्मत्वम् ॥ ३-३६ ॥
3.36 bhedatiraskāre sargāntarakarmatvam ||

In the disappearance of the act of distinction is the state of action of another creation of the world.

भेद bheda [m. TP cpd bheda-] *distinction, difference, kind, sort, species, variety; breaking, splitting, cleaving, tearing, piercing.* तिरस् tiras [ind.] *without, across, beyond; through; apart from, against; apart or secretly from; apart, secretly.* कारे kāre [m. loc. sg. -kāra] *(ifc.) in an act, action; in making, doing, working, a maker, doer (ifc.).* तिरस्कारे tiraskāre [m. loc. sg. TP cpd -tiraskāra] *in without the act -> in the disappearance of the act.* सर्ग sarga [m. sarga-] *creation of the world, emission or creation of matter, primary creation.* अन्तर antara [n. -antara] *(ifc.) another, different, other, being in the interior, interior.* कर्मत्वम् karmatvam [n. nom. sg. karmatva] *the state or effect of action.*

करणशक्तिः स्वतोऽनुभवात् ॥ ३-३७ ॥
3.37 karaṇaśaktiḥ svato'nubhavāt ||
The power of producing is from one's own experience.

करण karaṇa [n.] *the act of producing, making, doing, effecting; an act, deed.* शक्तिः śaktiḥ [f. nom. sg. TP cpd -śakti] *power, strength, might, energy, ability, capability, effort; faculty, skill, capacity for.* स्वतः svataḥ [ind. sva-tas] *of one's own self, of one's own accord.* अनुभवात् anubhavāt [m. abl. sg. anu-bhava] *from or through experience, knowledge derived from personal observation or experiment.*

त्रिपदाद्यनुप्राणनम् ॥ ३-३८ ॥
3.38 tripadādyanuprāṇanam ||
Beginnings of the three parts is after the act of animating.

त्रिपद tripada *having three parts (waking, dream and deep sleep), portions, divisions; three-footed.* आदि ādi [m.] *beginnings, (ifc.) beginning with, et caetera.* अनु anu [ind.] *(as a prefix to verbs and nouns, expresses) after, along, near to, under, with.* प्राणनम् prāṇanam [n. nom. sg. prāṇana] *the act of animating or vivifying; breathing, respiration.*

चित्तस्थितिवच्छरीरकरणबाह्येषु ॥ ३-३९ ॥
3.39 cittasthitivac charīrakaraṇabāhyeṣu ||
In the outer of the organs of sense of the body is like being in a state of mind.

चित्त citta [n. TP cpd citta-] *the mind, heart; thinking, reflecting, imagining, thought.* स्थिति sthiti [f. -sthiti-] *being or staying or remaining in any state or condition, standing, remaining, stay.* वत् vat *an affix added to words to imply likeness or resemblance; like, as.* शरीर śarīra [n. śarīra-] *the body, bodily frame, solid parts of the body.* करण karaṇa [n. -karaṇa-] *an organ of sense, an instrument, a means of action; the act of making, doing, producing, effecting; an act, deed.* बाह्येषु bāhyeṣu [m./n. loc. pl. -bāhya] *in the outer, exterior; in not belonging to the family or country, strange, foreign, outcaste; diverging from, conflicting with, opposed to.*

अभिलापाद्बहिर्गतिः संवाह्यस्य ॥ ३-४० ॥
3.40 abhilāpād bahirgatiḥ saṃvāhyasya ||
From expression is the extroversion of the "to be carried."

अभिलापात् abhilāpāt [m. abl. sg. abhi-lāpa] *from expression, word.*[1] बहिर्गतिः bahirgatiḥ [f. nom. sg. bahir-gati] *outwards going, extroversion.* बहिर् bahir [ind. in cpd for bahis] *out, forth, outwards, outside.* गतिः gatiḥ [f. nom. sg. gati] *going, moving, motion in general; path, way; state, condition; mode of existence.* संवाह्यस्य saṃvāhyasya [m. gen. sg. saṃvāhya] *of the to be carried or borne.*

तदारूढप्रमितेस्तत्क्षयाज्जीवसंक्षयः ॥ ३-४१ ॥
3.41 tadārūḍhapramites tatkṣayāj jīvasaṃkṣayaḥ ||
From the destruction of this world, of the manifestation brought to this world, is the complete destruction of life.

तत् tat [n. nom. sg. tad-] *this world; it, that, this.* आरूढ ārūḍha *brought to (often used in compounds), reached; having reached or attained, come into (a state); raised up, elevated on high.* प्रमितेः pramiteḥ [f. abl./gen. sg. pra-miti] *of the manifestation from/of correct notion, right conception,*

[1] Other versions of the śivasūtra write abhilāsāt [m. abl. sg. abhi-lāsa] *from desire.*

knowledge gained or established by proof. तत् tat [n. nom. sg. tad-] *it, that, this; this world.* क्षयात् kṣayāt [m. abl. sg. kṣaya] *from the destruction, loss, waste, diminution, decay.* जीव jīva [m.] *life, existence; living, existing, alive; any living being; the principle of life, vital breath, the living or personal soul.* संक्षयः saṃkṣayaḥ [m. nom. sg. saṃ-kṣaya] *complete destruction or consumption, wasting, decay, disappearance; the dissolution of all things, destruction of the world.*

भूतकञ्चुकी तदा विमुक्तो भूयः पतिसमः परः ॥ ३-४२ ॥
3.42 bhūtakañcukī tadā vimukto bhūyaḥ patisamaḥ paraḥ ||
The snake of the world, which has recently cast its skin, is then again like the supreme Lord.

भूत bhūta [n.] *that which is or exists, any living being, the world; a spirit, a demon; an element; the past; reality, fact, an actual occurrence.* कञ्चुकी kañcukī [m. nom. sg. -kañcukin] *having a garment, covered with, wrapped up in; mailed; furnished with armor or mail.* [m.] *a snake, an attendant on the woman's apartments, a chamberlain.* तदा tadā [ind.] *then, at that time, in that case.* विमुक्तः vimuktaḥ [m. nom. sg. -vimukta] *(a snake) which has recently cast its skin; freed or delivered or escaped from, set free, liberated (esp.) from mundane existence.* भूयः bhūyaḥ [ind. in cpd for bhūyas-] *again, once more; more, more numerous or abundant, greater, larger, mightier; most, very much, exceedingly; still more, moreover, besides, further on.* पति pati [m.] *a lord, master, owner, possessor, ruler, sovereign.* समः samaḥ [m. nom. sg. sama] *like, same, equal, similar.* परः paraḥ [m. nom. sg. para] *supreme, highest, chief; beyond.*
(Note: Choosing for bhūtakañcukī *having a garment of elements* instead of *the snake of the world* 3.42 might be translated as *Freed again from having a garment of elements is then like the supreme Lord.*)

नैसर्गिकः प्राणसम्बन्धः ॥ ३-४३ ॥
3.43 naisargikaḥ prāṇasambandhaḥ ||
The connection with the breath of life is inherent.

नैसर्गिकः naisargikaḥ [m. nom. sg. naiḥsargika] *inherent, natural, inborn, innate, original.* प्राण prāṇa [m.] *the breath of life, breath, respiration, spirit, vitality; vigor, energy, power; a vital organ, vital air.* सम्बन्धः

sambandhaḥ [m. nom. sg. sambandha] *connection with or related to; binding or joining together, close connection or union or association, conjunction; relationship, friendship.*

नासिकान्तर्मध्यसंयमात्किमत्र सव्यापसव्यसौषुम्नेषु ॥ ३-४४ ॥
3.44 nāsikāntarmadhyasaṃyamāt kim atra
savyāpasavyasauṣumneṣu ||
From the control of the senses of the internal middle of the nose, what is in this respect in the susumna channels on the left and right?

नासिका nāsikā [f.] *the nose; a nostril.* अन्तर् antar [ind. antar-] *(ibc.) internal, interior, intermediate; within, between, amongst, in the middle or interior.* मध्य madhya [n. -madhya] *in the middle, midst, center, inside, interior; in the middle of the sky, in the space between.* संयमात् saṃyamāt [m. abl. sg. saṃyama] *from control (esp.) control of the senses, holding together, restraint, self-control.* किम् kim [ind.] *what?, how?, whence?, wherefore?, why?* अत्र atra [ind.] *in this respect, in this matter.* सव्य savya [n.] *(ibc.) on the left; left, left hand.* अपसव्य apasavya [apa-savya] *right, not on the left side; (with auguries) from the right to the left, moving to the left.* सौषुम्ने सु sauṣumneṣu [n. loc. pl. from su-ṣumṇa] *in the susumna channels (veins in the body for prana called ida, susumna, pingala); in very favorable, benevolent, gracious or kind.*

भूयः स्यात्प्रतिमीलनम् ॥ ३-४५ ॥
3.45 bhūyaḥ syāt pratimīlanam ||
Again one should be towards closing the eyes.

भूयः bhūyaḥ [ind. in cpd for bhūyas-] *again, once more; moreover, still more, besides, further on; most, very much, exceedingly.* स्यात् syāt [3rd sg. pr. opt. act. √as] *one should be, may one be.* प्रति prati [ind.] *(as a prefix to nouns it expresses) towards, near to; likeness or comparison.* मीलनम् mīlanam [n. nom. sg. mīlana] *the act of closing the eyes; closing (said of eyes and flowers).*

śivasūtra

The Shiva Sutra

in English

The Shiva Sutra

Note that in a translation of Sanskrit into English, particles (*the* or *a*) and implied forms of the verb "to be" (*is* or *are*) are added due to Western grammatical requirements. Also, Sanskrit has no distinction between lower and upper case (*self* or *Self*). You might want to take this into account and consider an even more literal translation of the Sutra for your meditation by honoring the timelessness of the nominal sentence structure of the aphorisms by not adding "is" in the English translation of the aphorisms, for example:

1.1 *Consciousness – Self*, 1.2 *Knowledge – bondage*, and so on.

1 The way of Shiva

1.1 Consciousness is Self.

1.2 Knowledge is bondage.

1.3 The multitude of similar origins is the body of parts of the whole.

1.4 The basis of knowledge is an alphabet.

1.5 Zeal is Bhairava.

1.6 In union of multitude of powers is destruction of the universe.

1.7 In the distinction of deep sleep, dreaming and waking is the source of fullness of the Fourth.

1.8 Knowledge is waking.

1.9 Dreaming – imaginations.

1.10 Non-distinction is deep sleep, which is Maya.

1.11 The Eater of the triad is Shiva.
or: The Enjoyer of the triad is Shiva.

1.12 The stages of yoga are a wonder.

1.13 Desire, power is Uma, the Virgin.

1.14 Any visible object is a body.

1.15 From the union of the mind in the heart is the appearance of dreams of any visible object.

1.16 Or from the union with the Pure Principle without the power of animals.

1.17 Reflection is knowledge of the self.

1.18 Pure happiness of the world is joy of contemplation.

1.19 In the union of power is the origin of bodies.

1.20 Union of elements, separateness of elements, and all-pervading union.

1.21 Fulfilment of being the lord of the world is from rising of pure knowledge.

1.22 From investigation of the great deep water is the experience of the energy of mantras.

2 The way of the competent one

2.1 Mind is a mantra.

2.2 Persevering effort is fulfilling.

2.3 The being of the body of knowledge is the secret of a mantra.

2.4 Development of the mind in the womb is a dream of indistinct knowledge.

2.5 Flying the state of Shiva is in the rising of knowledge arising from one's own nature.

2.6 The guru is the means.

2.7 Perfect knowledge of the multitude of letters.

2.8 The body is an oblation.

2.9 Knowledge is food.

2.10 In the destruction of knowledge is the appearance of dreaming of a coming forth of That.

3 The fine way

3.1 The self is mind.

3.2 Knowledge is bondage.

3.3 Of the beginnings of any single part of the whole is non-distinction of realities, which is Maya.

3.4 The destroyer of parts is in a body.

3.5 The accumulation of channels, victory over the elements, detachment of the elements, and separateness of the elements.

3.6 Fulfilment is from an act of concealing the delusion of mind.

3.7 Through the conquest of the delusion of mind, through infinite enjoyment is the conquest of natural knowledge.

3.8 Waking is the doer of forming the second part of anything.

3.9 The dancer is Self.

3.10 The stage is the inner self.

3.11 The spectators are the organs of sense.

3.12 By means of wisdom is fulfilment of true essence.

3.13 One who has attained the highest truth is a free being.

3.14 As there so elsewhere.

3.15 Attention of origin.

3.16 Practising asana he easily immerses in deep water.

3.17 One causes the creation of one's own measure.

3.18 Not in the destruction of knowledge is the destruction of birth.

3.19 The Energy of Shiva et caetera in the beginnings of the class of gutteral letters are the mothers of animals.

3.20 The Fourth should be poured like oil in the Three.

3.21 One should enter with one's own mind immerged.

3.22 Within the practice of prana is a looking on all with indifferent eyes.

3.23 Inferior generation in the space between.

3.24 In the act of uniting one's own conception of measures is the act of rising again of the lost.

3.25 He becomes like Shiva.

3.26 Maintenance of the body is a holy practice.

3.27 Conversation is mantra recitation.

3.28 The act of giving is self-knowledge.

3.29 He who is engaged in guarding sheep and the cause of knowing.

3.30 The multitude of his own power is all-pervading.

3.31 Maintenance of life and dissolution.

3.32 Also without exclusion, this world and acting are both from the character of one who has consciousness.

3.33 Pleasure and pain is outwards thinking.

3.34 But freed from this world is one devoted to the doctrine of the absolute unity of spirit.

3.35 But one whose character is action is towards forming one mass of delusion.

3.36 In the disappearance of the act of distinction is the state of action of another creation of the world.

3.37 The power of producing is from one's own experience.

3.38 Beginnings of the three parts is after the act of animating.

3.39 In the outer of the organs of sense of the body is like being in a state of mind.

3.40 From expression is the extroversion of the "to be carried."

3.41 From the destruction of this world, of the manifestation brought to this world, is the complete destruction of life.

3.42 The snake of the world, which has recently cast its skin, is then again like the supreme Lord.
or: Freed again from having a garment of elements is then like the supreme Lord.

3.43 The connection with the breath of life is inherent.

3.44 From the control of the senses of the internal middle of the nose, what is in this respect in the susumna channels on the left and right?

3.45 Again one should be towards closing the eyes.

Printed in the USA
CPSIA information can be obtained
at www.ICGtesting.com
LVHW032141090923
757755LV00005B/110

9 789078 623144